The Wild Rabbit

By Oxford Scientific Films

Photographs by George Bernard

G.P. Putnam's Sons   New York

First American Edition 1980
Text/Nature's Way copyright © 1980 by G. Whizzard Publications Ltd.
Photographs copyright © 1980 by Oxford Scientific Films Ltd.
All rights reserved.
Printed in Belgium by Proost, Turnhout

Library of Congress Cataloging in Publication Data
Oxford Scientific Films.
The wild rabbit.
SUMMARY: Describes the physical characteristics and
habits of the wild European rabbit
which is found on every continent.
1. Oryctolagus cuniculus – Juvenile literature.
[1. European rabbits. 2. Rabbits]
I. Bernard, George. II. Title.
QL737.L32093 1980   599'.322   79-26522
ISBN 0-399-20730-9

The Wild Rabbit

The wild European rabbit (*Oryctolagus cuniculus*) originally came from the western Mediterranean. It spread into central Europe, and later was introduced into Australia, New Zealand, North Africa, North and South America, and Asia. The rabbit is often confused with its relative the hare, although the two animals seldom mix. Hares are much bigger, with longer hind legs and larger ears. Unlike the rabbit, they do not burrow and their young are born above ground.

A fully grown rabbit measures about 40-45 cm (16-18 in) and weighs up to 2 kg ($4\frac{1}{2}$ lb). It has thick brownish-grey fur, white underparts, and a short, upturned tail, or scut. There is little difference in size between the doe (female) and the buck (male), but the latter has a broader head. The rabbit's eyesight is not exceptional but its long pointed ears provide it with excellent hearing. Its sense of smell is equally strong. Just in front of the nostrils, are two small sensing pads loosely covered with hairy flaps of skin which are used for detecting and identifying smells, such as food and other animals. The characteristic twitching of the rabbit's nostrils opens and closes the flaps, exposing the pads to the air.

Providing climate and conditions are not extreme, rabbits can live almost anywhere, digging their burrows on farmland, sand dunes, salt marshes, open woodland and moorland, hillsides and cliffs. They are very social animals and live in colonies in an underground network of burrows and tunnels, called a warren.

It is the doe, not the buck, that does the hard work of building the warren. Using her forepaws she cuts deeper and deeper into the soil, kicking the dirt out under her tail. The tunnels are usually made about 15 cm (6 in) high, large enough for a rabbit to move through with ease. They vary considerably in length with some as long as 30 m (100 ft), and they can be as deep as 2.7 m (9 ft) underground. The warren normally has a number of entrances and several escape holes — small openings, about 6 cm ($2\frac{1}{2}$ in) high, just big enough for the rabbit to squeeze through in an emergency.

The same warren may be used by generations of rabbits over several years; some are known to have been occupied for as long as thirty or forty years. A warren can be relatively small, 40 square meters (370 sq ft) or so, or stretch across 40 hectares (100 acres). The size of the colony is equally varied, with less than a dozen rabbits in some and many hundreds in others.

Rabbits can breed at any time of the year, but the main breeding season is for a period of five to six months from the beginning of winter through to early summer. A buck will mate with several does during this time, but he takes no part in rearing the young. The baby rabbits are called kittens. A litter averages three to six kittens, born about four weeks after mating.

A doe can produce a litter roughly every thirty days, because she can mate again within two days of giving birth. However, many of the embryos (unborn kittens) die at an early stage of the pregnancy and by a special process are reabsorbed into the doe's body system. This tends to happen when the animal is under stress, perhaps through overcrowding or lack of food. However, a healthy doe normally gives birth to about ten live kittens a year.

The buck and doe go through a kind of courtship dance before mating, excitedly running around in circles. The doe flicks her tail as she leaps about, then squats down and lifts her hindquarters. The buck mounts her from behind and with rapid thrusting movements places his sperm inside her. The mating is now completed, although the rabbits may repeat the act several times before finally parting.

The pregnant doe sets about making a home for her new family. She digs a nest burrow, called a stop, and shortly before giving birth lines it with grass or straw, and fur from her body. The stop may be either a short extension of the main warren, some 60-90 cm (2-3 ft) long, or an entirely separate burrow. The latter will sometimes be the starting point for a new colony.

The young rabbits are born below ground, eyes closed, ears undeveloped and body without fur. At this stage they weigh less than 56 gms (2 oz). The doe visits the stop once a day to nurse them. When she leaves she covers the entrance with earth to conserve heat and hide the burrow. The kittens can crawl at birth and during the first few days frequently make little jumping movements, falling about on top of one another. It is thought that these "jumps" are the baby rabbit instinctively searching for its mother's teats to suckle.

The kitten develops quickly. After four days its fur is growing and, although It can't see, it reacts to sound. By the end of the first week, the kitten has doubled its weight and its teeth and claws are visible. Its eyes open about the tenth day.

The kittens grow increasingly restless in the stop, and during the third week they come out into the open to graze for the first time. In the beginning they stay close to the burrow entrance, going inside at the first sign of danger. The doe watches closely over her family, ready to sound the alarm by stamping her hind feet and raising her white tail.

Each day the young ones gain confidence and extend the range of their activities. They learn how to make use of cover, when to stay still and when to run. Then, in the fourth week, the doe leaves them to prepare for her next litter. The young rabbits are on their own to fend for themselves.

If the warren is not too crowded the young rabbits will probably stay close to the colony, taking over an empty burrow. Sometimes, however, they are driven out by older, hostile rabbits and have to find a new home elsewhere. Generally, young bucks are more inclined to travel than does.

Rabbits reach adult size at about nine months. Does can breed after five months but bucks are not usually ready to mate until they are almost a year old. Toward the end of summer, rabbits moult. Their fur is thinned out and replaced by a thicker, warmer winter coat. Rabbits rarely breed during the moulting period, but with the onset of winter they are ready to start again.

Rabbits are vegetarians with big appetites, eating a pound or more of fresh green food every day when they can get it. Grass, leafy plants, cereals, roots, and the bark of young trees all contribute to their diet. They also love vegetables like carrots, lettuce, and peas. The rabbit has two kinds of teeth: sharp, chisel-like incisors at the front for cutting, and molars at the back for grinding. As the incisors never stop growing, the rabbit must constantly gnaw at plants and trees to keep them worn down.

At dawn and dusk, rabbits emerge from the safety

of the warren to feed. They do this by a process known as refection, which is similar in some ways to cattle chewing their cud. Rabbits eat rapidly and in large quantities. Then, while the rabbit is resting in its burrow during the day, it excretes food in a semi-digested form as soft, moist pellets. These are eaten immediately by the rabbit and pass through its system again to be fully digested. The rabbit droppings that are seen lying on the ground are the second, dry pellets that the animal excretes.

In between grazing, rabbits love to play together, to explore, to bask in the sun, and to groom themselves. But they are not always friendly to each other. Using their sharp claws and teeth, bucks will fight over does, particularly during the breeding season, and to defend their territory from outsiders. The fights are often fierce, and occasionally to the death.

One of the ways a buck marks its territory is by "chinning." Just below its jaw the rabbit has special glands which produce a colorless scented fluid. The rabbit lays its scent by rubbing its chin on the ground or on a plant. Although both does and bucks have these glands, chinning is predominantly a male habit.

Rabbits have many enemies. On the ground, there are foxes, badgers, dogs, cats, ferrets, weasels, stoats, skunks, coyotes, wolves, and snakes; in the air, eagles, owls, hawks, and buzzards stalk them. Young rabbits in particular fall prey to many of these creatures, and the death-rate generally is high. Humans are an even worse enemy. Considered to be a pest because of the damage it does to farmland, crops, and trees, the rabbit is trapped, gassed, and shot on a wide scale.

But the animal's problems do not end there. Thousands of rabbits die of cold and hunger, and in recent years a disease called myxomatosis has killed millions of them in Europe and Australia. At one time almost the entire rabbit population of some countries was wiped out, but enough survived to carry on breeding and rabbits are once again on the increase.

Although wild rabbits can live for as long as ten years, the average age is nearer two. With so many enemies, it is just as well they breed often and easily.

Rabbits live underground in a network of burrows and tunnels called a warren.

The doe and the buck are about the same size, but the buck has a broader head.

The rabbit has a strong sense of smell.

It uses two special sensing pads in front of its nostrils to recognize different smells.

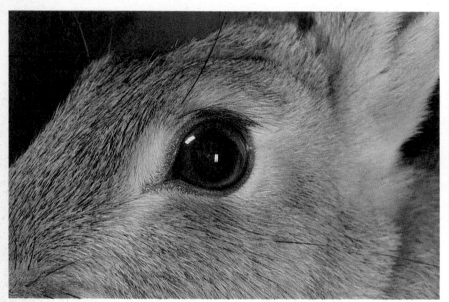

The rabbit has big round eyes and a white tail, which it raises to warn other rabbits of danger.

This rabbit is crouching outside one of the entrances to its warren.

The tunnels are just large enough for the rabbit to move through.

This buck finds a doe to mate with.

He chases her in a kind of dance and then they mate.

The doe collects grass for lining her nest.

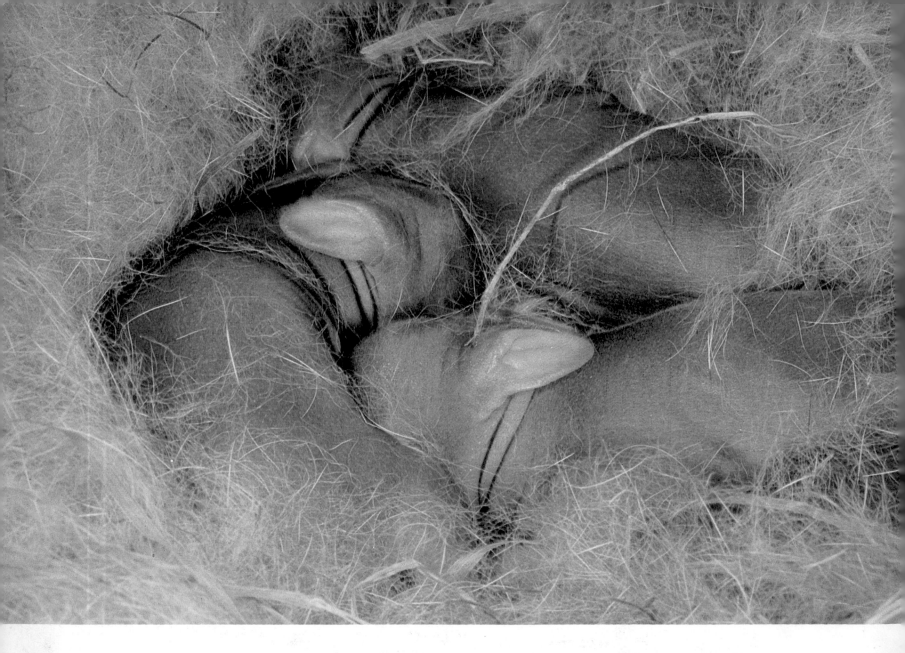

The one-day-old kittens have no fur, and they cannot see or hear.

After four days they have some fur and their ears are starting to develop, but their eyes are still closed.

Their eyes open about the tenth day. The kittens stay in the nest for

another week before coming above ground to graze for the first time.

This four-week-old rabbit grooms itself.

Near the end of summer, the rabbit sheds its fur and grows a thicker winter coat.

Rabbits eat lots of grass, plants, and roots as fast as they can. They also like fresh vegetables and cereals when they can get them.

Back in the safety of its burrow, the rabbit eats the soft, moist pellets of half-digested food which have passed through its body.

Bucks mark their territory by rubbing scent on plants or the ground with their chins.

Scraping the ground is another male habit.

Rabbits are curious and often stand on their hind legs to see.

They usually run away from danger.

But sometimes they stay still, hidden in the long grass.

Hiding in snow is more difficult.

Rabbits have many enemies, including people. This man will try to chase some rabbits out of their holes and into traps.

But, most of the time, a rabbit is safe inside its burrow.

Books by Oxford Scientific Films

BEES AND HONEY
Photographs by David Thompson

THE BUTTERFLY CYCLE
Photographs by Dr. John Cooke

HOUSE MOUSE
Photographs by David Thompson

THE SPIDER'S WEB
Photographs by Dr. John Cooke

THE STICKLEBACK CYCLE
Photographs by David Thompson

THE CHICKEN AND THE EGG
Photographs by George Bernard & Peter Parks

COMMON FROG
Photographs by George Bernard

DRAGONFLIES
Photographs by George Bernard

THE WILD RABBIT
Photographs by George Bernard